ßↄ

Angle of Ascent

Angle
of
Ascent

New

and

Selected

Poems

by

Robert Hayden

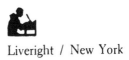

Liveright / New York

Library of Congress Cataloging in Publication Data

Hayden, Robert Earl.
  Angle of ascent.

  I. Title.
PS3515.A9363A6   1975   811'.5'2   75-20493

ISBN 13: 978-0-87140-106-9

In memory of
Roanne and Richard

Acknowledgments

Grateful acknowledgment is made
to the editors of the *Iowa Review*,
Periodical Lunch, and *World Order*
for permission to reprint poems
first published in these journals.

I wish to express my gratitude to
David Way, Paul Breman, and Leo B. Kneer
for their help and encouragement
over the years.

ß❧

Contents

III Words in the Mourning Time

IV A Ballad of Remembrance

I

Angle of Ascent

Beginnings

I

Plowdens, Finns,
Sheffeys, Haydens,
Westerfields.

Pennsylvania gothic,
Kentucky homespun,
Virginia baroque.

II
A shotgun on his shoulder,
his woman big with child and
shrieking curses after him,

Joe Finn came down from
Allegheny wilderness
to join Abe Lincoln's men.

Goddamning it survives the
slaughter at the Crater.
Disappears into his name.

III

Greatgrandma Easter, on my father's side,
was a Virginia freedman's Indian bride.
She was more than six feet tall. At ninety could
still chop and tote firewood.

IV

Great-aunt Sally, great-aunt Melisse—
how they danced and sang in that hoo-rah's house.
Sold their parlor chairs to go
to Billy Kersands' minstrel show;
crooned and shuffled when they came back home,
Brother Tambo, Brother Bones.

Melissabelle and Sarah Jane
oh they took all the prizes one Hallowe'en.
And we'll let the calico curtain fall
on Pochahontas and the Corncob Queen
dancing the figures the callers call—
Sashay, ladies, promenade, all.

V
(The Crystal Cave Elegy)

Floyd Collins oh
I guess he's a goner,
Pa Hayden sighed,
the Extra trembling
in his hands.
Poor game loner
trapped in the rock
of Crystal Cave, as
once in Kentucky coal-
mine dark (I taste the
darkness yet)
my greenhorn dream of
life. Alive down there
in his grave. Open
for him, blue door.

Free Fantasia: Tiger Flowers
(for Michael)

The sporting people
along St. Antoine—
that scufflers'
paradise of ironies—
        bet salty money
on his righteous
        hook and jab.

I was a boy then, running
(unbeknownst to Pa)
errands for Miss Jackie
and Stack-o'-Diamonds' Eula Mae.
. . . Their perfumes,
rouged Egyptian faces.
        Their pianolas jazzing.

O Creole babies,
Dixie odalisques,
speeding through cutglass
dark to see the macho angel
        trick you'd never
turn, his bluesteel prowess
        in the ring.

Hardshell believers
amen'd the wreck
as God A'mighty's
will. I'd thought
        such gaiety could not
die. Nor could our
        elegant avenger.

The Virgin Forest
by Rousseau—
its psychedelic flowers
towering, its deathless
        dark dream figure
death the leopard
        claws—I choose it
now as elegy
        for Tiger Flowers.

For a Young Artist

Sprawled in the pigsty,
      snouts nudging snuffling him—
a naked old man
      with bloodstained wings.

      Fallen from the August sky?
Dead? Alive?
      But he twists away

from the cattle-prod, wings
      jerking, lifts his grizzled head,
regarding all
      with searching eyes.

Neither smiles nor threats,
dumbshow nor lingua franca
were of any use to those
trying for clues to him.

They could not make him hide
his nakedness
in their faded hand-me-downs.

Humane, if hostile and afraid,
they spread him a pallet
in the chicken-house.
The rooster pecked his wings.

Leftovers were set out for him;
he ate sunflowers
instead and the lice crawling his feathers.

Carloads of the curious paid
his clever hosts to see the
actual angel? carny freak?
in the barbedwire pen.

They crossed themselves and prayed
his blessing;
catcalled and chunked at him.

In the dark his heavy wings
open and shut, stiffly spread
    like a wooden butterfly's.

He leaps, board wings clum-
sily flapping, big sex
    flopping, falls.

The hawk-haunted fowl
flutter and squawk;
    panic squeals in the sty.

He strains, an awk-
ward patsy, sweating strains
    leaping falling. Then—

    silken rustling in the air,
the angle of ascent
    achieved.

(After the story, "A Very old Man with Enormous Wings,"
by Gabriel García Márques)

Stars

I
Stood there then among
spears and kindled shields,
    praising Orion.

II
Betelgeuse Aldebaran

Abstract as future yesterdays
        the starlight
crosses eons of meta-space
        to us.

    Algol Arcturus Almaak

How shall the mind keep warm
        save at spectral
fires—how thrive but by the light
        of paradox?

    Altair Vega Polaris Maia

III
(Sojourner Truth)

Comes walking barefoot
out of slavery

ancestress
childless mother

following the stars
her mind a star

IV
Pulsars, blue receding
quasars—their vibrant
radio waves.
       Cosmic Ouija,
what is the
mathematics of your message?

V
(The Nine-Pointed Star)

Stable stars, variable stars—
hydrogen-into-helium
fusions, radiations, spectral fires.

And the Nine-Pointed Star,
sun star in the constellation
of the nuclear Will;

fixed star whose radiance
filtering down to us lights mind and
spirit, signals future light.

Two Egyptian Portrait Masks

1. Nefert-iti

A memory
carved on stelae of
the city Akhenaten built for God—

      Fair of face Joyous with the Double Plume
      Mistress of Happiness   Endowed
      with Favor   at hearing whose Voice

      one rejoices   Lady of Grace
      Great of Love   whose disposition cheers
      the Lord of Two Lands—

whose burntout
loveliness alive in stone
is like the fire of precious stones

dynastic
death (gold mask and vulture wings)
charmed her with so she would never die.

II. *Akhenaten*

Upon the
mountain Aten spoke
and set the spirit moving

in the
Pharaoh's heart: O Lord of every land
shining forth for all:

Aten
multi-single like the sun
reflecting Him by Him

reflected.
Anubis howled. The royal prophet reeled
under the dazzling weight

of vision,
exalted—maddened?—the spirit moving
in his heart: Aten Jahveh Allah God.

Butterfly Piece
  (for Robert Stilwell)

Brazilian butterflies, static and perfect as
        enamelwork by Fabergé. Jewel corpses fixed
in glass. Black opal flowerskin banded
        neargold yellow; sea-agate striped berylgreen;

        Colors so intense I imagine them heavy enough
                to have broken the live wings—as human
        colors in our inhuman world burden, break.

                Occult prismatic blue of the Morpho,
                        the great prized Morpho that living seems
                conjured forth by magic hands. Wild beauty
                        killed, sold to prettify.

The Moose Wallow

Friends warned of moose that
often came to the wallow
near the path I took.

I feared, hoped to see
the tall ungainly creatures
in their battle crowns.

I felt their presence
in the dark (hidden watchers)
on either side.

Crispus Attucks

Name in a footnote. Faceless name.
Moot hero shrouded in Betsy Ross
and Garvey flags—propped up
by bayonets, forever falling.

II

The Night-Blooming

Cereus

Richard Hunt's "Arachne"

Human face becoming locked insect face
        mouth of agony shaping a cry it cannot utter
            eyes bulging brimming with the horrors
                of her becoming

            Dazed crazed
        by godly vivisection husking her
    gutting her
cutting hubris its fat and bones away

In goggling terror fleeing powerless to flee
        Arachne not yet arachnid and no longer woman
            in the moment's centrifuge of dying
                becoming

The Night-Blooming Cereus

And so for nights
we waited, hoping to see
the heavy bud
  break into flower.

On its neck-like tube
hooking down from the edge
of the leaf-branch
  nearly to the floor,

the bud packed
tight with its miracle swayed
stiffly on breaths
  of air, moved

as though impelled
by stirrings within itself.
It repelled as much
  as it fascinated me

sometimes—snake,
eyeless bird head,
beak that would gape
  with grotesque life-squawk.

But you, my dear,
conceded less to the bizarre
than to the imminence
  of bloom. Yet we agreed

we ought
to celebrate the blossom,
paint ourselves, dance
  in honor of

archaic mysteries
when it appeared. Meanwhile
we waited, aware
        of rigorous design.

    Backster's
polygraph, I thought,
would have shown
        (as clearly as it had

    a philodendron's
fear) tribal sentience
in the cactus, focused
        energy of will.

    That belling of
tropic perfume—that
signalling
        not meant for us;

    the darkness
cloyed with summoning
fragrance. We dropped
        trivial tasks

    and marvelling
beheld at last the achieved
flower. Its moonlight
        petals were

    still unfold-
ing, the spike fringe of the outer
perianth recessing
        as we watched.

Lunar presence,
foredoomed, already dying,
it charged the room
        with plangency

        older than human
cries, ancient as prayers
invoking Osiris, Krishna,
        Tezcátlipóca.

        We spoke
in whispers when
we spoke
        at all . . .

The Performers

Easily, almost matter-of-factly they step,
two minor Wallendas, with pail and squeegee along
the wintry ledge, hook their harness to the wall
and leaning back into a seven-story angle of space
begin washing the office windows. I
am up there too until straps break
and iron paper apple of iron I fall
through plateglass wind onto stalagmites below.

But am safely at my desk again by the time
the hairline walkers, high-edge
balancers end their center-ring routine
and crawl inside. A rough day, I remark,
for such a risky business. Many thanks.
Thank *you*, sir, one of the men replies.

The Peacock Room
(in memory of Betsy Graves Reyneau)

Ars Longa   Which is crueller
Vita Brevis   life or art?
     Thoughts in the Peacock Room,
where briefly I shelter. As in the glow
(remembered or imagined?)
     of the lamp shaped like a rose
my mother would light
for me some nights to keep
     Raw-Head-And-Bloody-Bones away.

Exotic, fin de siècle, unreal
and beautiful the Peacock Room.
     Triste metaphor.
Hiroshima   Watts   My Lai.
Thus history scorns
     the vision chambered in gold
and Spanish leather, lyric space;
rebukes, yet cannot give the lie
     to what is havened here.

Environment as ornament.
Whistler with arrogant art designed
     it, mocking a connoisseur
with satiric arabesque of gold
peacocks on a wall peacock blue
     in fury trampling coins of gold.
Such vengeful harmonies drove
a rival mad. As in a dream
     I see the crazed young man.

He shudders in a corner, shields
his face in terror of
        the perfect malice of those claws.
She too is here—ghost
of the happy child she was that day.
        When I turned twelve,
they gave me for a birthday gift
a party in the Peacock Room.
        With shadow cries

the peacocks flutter down,
their spread tails concealing her,
        then folding, drooping to reveal
her eyeless, old—Med School
cadaver, flesh-object
        pickled in formaldehyde,
who was artist, compassionate,
clear-eyed. Who was belovéd friend.
        No more. No more.

The birds resume their splendored pose.
And Whistler's portrait of
        a tycoon's daughter gleams
like imagined flowers. What is art?
What is life?
        What the Peacock Room?
Rose-leaves and ashes drift
its portals, gently spinning toward
        a bronze Bodhisattva's ancient smile.

Smelt Fishing

I

In the cold spring night
the smelt are spawning. Sportsmen
fevered crowd the lake.

II

Thin snow scatters on
the wind, melting as it falls.
Cries for help for light.

III

Who is he night-
waters entangle, reclaim?
Blank fish-eyes.

"Dance the Orange"
(Rilke)

And dance this
boneharp tree

and dance this
boneflower tree

tree in the
snowlight

miming a dancer
dancing a tree

Traveling through Fog

Looking back, we cannot see,
except for its blurring lights
like underwater stars and moons,
our starting-place.
Behind us, beyond us now
is phantom territory, a world
abstract as memories of earth
the traveling dead take home.
Between obscuring cloud
and cloud, the cloudy dark
ensphering us seems all we can
be certain of. Is Plato's cave.

III

Words in the

Mourning Time

&

Sphinx

      If he could solve the riddle,
she would not leap
      from those gaunt rocks to her death,
but devour him instead.

      It pleasures her to hold
him captive there—
      to keep him in the reach of her
blood-matted paws.

      It is your fate, she has often
said, to endure
      my riddling. Your fate to live
at the mercy of my

      conundrum, which, in truth,
is only a kind
      of psychic joke. No, you shall
not leave this place.

      (Consider anyway the view from
here.) In time,
      you will come to regard my questioning
with a certain pained

      amusement; in time, get so
you would hardly find
      it possible to live without
my joke and me.

The Dream
(1863)

That evening Sinda thought she heard the drums
and hobbled from her cabin to the yard.
The quarters now were lonely-still in willow dusk
after the morning's ragged jubilo,
when laughing crying singing the folks went off
with Marse Lincum's soldier boys.
But Sinda hiding would not follow them: those
Buckras with their ornery
funning, cussed commands, oh they were not were not
the hosts the dream had promised her.

and hope when these few lines reaches your hand they
will fine you well. I am tired some but it is war you
know and ole jeff Davis muss be ketch an hung to a sour
apple tree like it says in the song I seen some akshun
but that is what i listed for not to see the sights ha ha
More of our peoples coming every day. the Kernul calls
them contrybans and has them work aroun the Camp
and learning to be soljurs. How is the wether home. Its
warm this evening but theres been lots of rain

How many times that dream had come to her—
more vision than a dream—
the great big soldiers marching out of gunburst,
their faces those of Cal and Joe
and Charlie sold to the ricefields oh sold away
a-many and a-many a long year ago.
Fevered, gasping, Sinda listened, knew this was
the ending of her dream and prayed
that death, grown fretful and impatient, nagging her,
would wait a little longer, would let her see.

and we been marching sleeping too in cold rain and
mirey mud a heap a times. Tell Mama Thanks for The
Bible an not worry so. Did brother fix the roof yet like
he promised? this mus of been a real nice place befor the
fighting uglied it all up the judas trees is blosommed out
so pretty same as if this hurt and truble wasnt going on.
Almos like somthing you mite dream about i take it for
a sign The Lord remembers Us Theres talk we will be
moving into Battle very soon agin

    Trembling tottering Hep me Jesus Sinda crossed
the wavering yard, reached
    a redbud tree in bloom, could go no farther, clung
to the bole and clinging fell
    to her knees. She tried to stand, could not so much
as lift her head, tried to hold
    the bannering sounds, heard only the whipoorwills
in tenuous moonlight; struggled to rise
    and make her way to the road to welcome Joe and Cal
and Charlie, fought with brittle strength to rise.

So pray for me that if the Bullit with my name rote on
it get me it will not get me in retreet i do not think them
kine of thots so much no need in Dying till you die I all
ways figger, course if the hardtack and the bullybeef do
not kill me nuthing can i guess. Tell Joe I hav shure
seen me some ficety gals down here in Dixieland & i
mite jus go ahead an jump over the broomstick with one
and bring her home, well I muss close with Love to all
& hope to see you soon Yrs Cal

" 'Mystery Boy' Looks for Kin in Nashville"

Puzzle faces in the dying elms
promise him treats if he will stay.
Sometimes they hiss and spit at him
like varmints caught
in a thicket of butterflies.

A black doll,
one disremembered time,
came floating down to him
through mimosa's fancywork leaves and blooms
to be his hidden bride.

From the road beyond the creepered walls
they call to him now and then,
and he'll take off in spite of the angry trees,
hearing like the loudening of his heart
the name he never can he never can repeat.

And when he gets to where the voices were—
Don't cry, his dollbaby wife implores;
I know where they are, don't cry.
We'll go and find them, we'll go
and ask them for your name again.

The Broken Dark

Sleepless, I stare
from the dark hospital room
at shadows of a flower and its leaves
the nightlight fixes like a blotto
on the corridor wall. Shadow-plays
of Bali—demons move to the left,
gods, in their frangipani crowns
and gold, to the right.
Ah and my life
in the shadow of God's laser light—
shadow of deformed homunculus?
A fool's errand given by fools.
Son, go fetch a pint of pigeon's milk
from the drugstore and be quick.
Demons on the left. Death on either side,
the Rabbi said, the way of life between.
That groaning. Man with his belly slashed,
two-timing lover. Dying?
The nightnurse rustles by.
Struggles in the pit. I have come back
to tell thee of struggles in the pit.
Perhaps is dying.
Free of pain, my own death still
a theorem to be proved.
Alláh'u'Abbhá. O Healing Spirit,
Thy nearness our forgiving cure.

Soledad
(And I, I am no longer of that world)

Naked, he lies in the blinded room
chainsmoking, cradled by drugs, by jazz
as never by any lover's cradling flesh.

Miles Davis coolly blows for him:
O pena negra, sensual Flamenco blues;
the red clay foxfire voice of Lady Day

(lady of the pure black magnolias)
sobsings her sorrow and loss and fare you well,
dryweeps the pain his treacherous jailers

have released him from for awhile.
His fears and his unfinished self
await him down in the anywhere streets.

He hides on the dark side of the moon,
takes refuge in a stained-glass cell,
flies to a clockless country of crystal.

Only the ghost of Lady Day knows where
he is. Only the music. And he swings
oh swings: beyond complete immortal now.

Aunt Jemima of the Ocean Waves

I

Enacting someone's notion of themselves
(and me), The One And Only Aunt Jemima
and Kokimo The Dixie Dancing Fool
do a bally for the freak show.

I watch a moment, then move on,
pondering the logic that makes of them
(and me) confederates
of The Spider Girl, The Snake-skinned Man. . . .

Poor devils have to live somehow.

I cross the boardwalk to the beach,
lie in the sand and gaze beyond
the clutter at the sea.

II

Trouble you for a light?
I turn as Aunt Jemima settles down
beside me, her blue-rinsed hair
without the red bandanna now.

I hold the lighter to her cigarette.
Much obliged. Unmindful (perhaps)
of my embarrassment, she looks
at me and smiles: You sure

do favor a friend I used to have.
Guess that's why I bothered you
for a light. So much like him that I—
She pauses, watching white horses rush

to the shore. Way them big old waves
come slamming whooping in,
sometimes it's like they mean to smash
this no-good world to hell.

    Well, it could happen. A book I read—
Crossed that very ocean years ago.
London, Paris, Rome,
Constantinople too—I've seen them all.

Back when they billed me everywhere
as the Sepia High Stepper.
Crowned heads applauded me.
Years before your time. Years and years.

I wore me plenty diamonds then,
and counts or dukes or whatever they were
would fill my dressing room
with the costliest flowers. But of course

there was this one you resemble so.
Get me? The sweetest gentleman.
Dead before his time. Killed in the war
to save the world for another war.

High-stepping days for me
were over after that. Still I'm not one
to let grief idle me for long.
I went out with a mental act—

mind-reading—Mysteria From
The Mystic East—veils and beads
and telling suckers how to get
stolen rings and sweethearts back.

One night he was standing by my bed,
seen him plain as I see you,
and warned me without a single word:
Baby, quit playing with spiritual stuff.

So here I am, so here I am,
fake mammy to God's mistakes.
And that's the beauty part,
I mean, ain't that the beauty part.

She laughs, but I do not, knowing what
her laughter shields. And mocks.
I light another cigarette for her.
She smokes, not saying any more.

Scream of children in the surf,
adagios of sun and flashing foam,
the sexual glitter, oppressive fun. . . .
An antique etching comes to mind:

"The Sable Venus" naked on
a baroque Cellini shell—voluptuous
imago floating in the wake
of slave-ships on fantastic seas.

Jemima sighs, Reckon I'd best
be getting back. I help her up.
Don't you take no wooden nickels, hear?
Tin dimes neither. So long, pal.

Locus
(for Ralph)

Here redbuds like momentary trees
     of an illusionist;
here Cherokee rose, acacia, and mimosa;
here magnolias—totemic flowers
     wreathing legends of this place.
Here violent metamorphosis,
     with every blossom turning
deadly and memorial soldiers,
their sabres drawn, charging
     firewood shacks,
apartheid streets. Here wound-red earth
     and blinding cottonfields,
rock hills where sachems counseled,
where scouts gazed stealthily
     upon the glittering death march
of De Soto through Indian wilderness.
     Here mockingbird and
cottonmouth, fury of rivers.
Here swamp and trace and bayou
     where the runagate hid,
the devil with Spanish pistols rode.
     Here spareness, rankness, harsh
brilliances; beauty of what's hardbitten,
knotted, stinted, flourishing
     in despite, on thorny meagerness
thriving, twisting into grace.
     Here symbol houses
where the brutal dream lives out its lengthy
dying. Here the past, adored and
     unforgiven. Here the past—
soulscape, Old Testament battleground
of warring shades whose weapons kill.

On Lookout Mountain

I listen for the sounds of cannon, cries
vibrating still upon the air,
timeless echoes in echoic time—
imagine how they circle out and out

concentric with Kilroy's cries,
as beyond the tangent calm
of this midcentury morning he burns
or freezes in the warfare of our peace.

I gaze through layered light,
think of the death-for-foothold inching climb
of Union soldiers struggling up
the crackling mountainside.

And here where Sunday alpinists
pick views and souvenirs,
here daring choices stained
the clouds with dubious victory.

A world away, yet nearer than our hope
or our belief, the scions of that fighting climb
endless hills of war, amid war's peaks
and valleys broken, scattered fall.

Have done, have done. Behold how bright
upon the mountain the gadget feet
of trivia shine.
Oh, hear the stuffed gold eagle sing.

Kodachromes of the Island

1

Halfnaked children
met us singing for coins
at the swaybacked jetty.

Gold brooms had swept
the mist away, and
the island air was clear.

Parrot and zinnia
colors teemed
in thronging sunlight.

A young beggar greeted us
Dios se lo pague
with fingerless hands.

II
Out on the yellow
as pollen or sulphur
lake Indian fishermen,

naked torsos oiled with
sunlight, were casting
their mariposas.

On the landing, women
were cleaning a catch and
tossing the guts to

squealing piglets. A tawny
butterfly drunkenly circled
then lighted on offal.

III

Black turkeys children
dogs foraged and played
under drying fishnets.

Vendors urged laquerwork
and glazed angels
with candles between their wings.

Alien, at home—as always
everywhere—I roamed
the cobbled island,

and thought of Yeats,
his passionate search for
a theme. Sought mine.

Zeus over Redeye
(The Redstone Arsenal)

Enclave where new mythologies
of power come to birth—
where coralled energy and power breed
like prized man-eating animals.
Like dragon, hydra, basilisk.

Radar corollas and Holland tulips
the colors of Easter eggs
form vistas for the ironist.
Where elm, ailanthus, redbud grew
parabola and gantry rise.

In soaring stasis rocket missiles loom,
the cherished weapons named for Nike
(O headless armless Victory),
for Zeus, Apollo, Hercules—
eponyms of redeyed fury
greater, lesser than their own.

Ignorant outlander, mere civilian,
not sure always of what it is
I see, I walk with you among
these totems of our fire-breathing age,
question and question you,

who are at home in terra guarded like
a sacred phallic grove.
Your partial answers reassure
me less than they appall.
I feel as though invisible fuses were

burning all around us burning all
around us. Heat-quiverings twitch
danger's hypersensitive skin.
The very sunlight here seems flammable.
And shadows give
us no relieving shade.

Unidentified Flying Object

It's true Mattie Lee
has clean disappeared.
And shouldn't we notify
the sheriff? No use, Will
insists, no earthly use.

He was sleeping one off
under the trees that night,
he claims, and woke up when
the space-ship
landed—a silvery dome

with gassy-green and red-
hot-looking lights like eyes
that stared blinked stared.
Says he hid himself
in the bushes and watched,

shaking. Pretty soon
a hatch slides open, a ramp
glides forward like
a glowing tongue poked out.
And who or what is it

silently present there?
Same as if Will's
trying to peer through webs
and bars of gauzy glare
screening, distorting a shape

he sees yet cannot see.
But crazier than that
was when Mattie Lee
came running from her house
toward the thing.

She's wearing her sunflower hat
and the dress the lady she cooked
for gave her, and it's like
she's late for work the way
she scurries up the ramp.

And it seems to Will
that in its queer
shining, plain Mattie Lee's
transformed—is every teasing brown
he's ever wanted, never had.

He's fixing to shout, Come back,
Mattie Lee, come back;
but a heavy hand is over his mouth
when he hears her laugh
as she steps inside

without even a goodbye glance
around. The next Will knew,
the UFO rose in the air—
no blastoff roar, no flame,
he says—hung in the dark,

hovered, shimmered,
its eyes pulsing, then whirred
spiraling into the sky,
vanished as though
it had never been.

Will's tale anyhow.
All I'm certain of
is Mattie Lee's
nowhere to be found
and must have gone

off in a hurry. Left her doors
unlocked and the radio on
and a roast in the oven. Strange.
As for Will, he's a changed man,
not drinking nowadays and sad.

Mattie Lee's friends—
she's got no kinfolks, lived
alone—are worried, swear
Will was craving her
and she held herself too good

for him, being head of Mount
Nebo's usher board and such.
And some are hinting what I,
for one—well, never mind.
The talk is getting mean.

El-Hajj Malik El-Shabazz

(Malcolm X)
O masks and metamorphoses of Ahab, Native Son

I

The icy evil that struck his father down
and ravished his mother into madness
trapped him in violence of a punished self
struggling to break free.

As Home Boy, as Dee-troit Red,
he fled his name, became the quarry of
his own obsessed pursuit.

He conked his hair and Lindy-hopped,
zoot-suited jiver, swinging those chicks
in the hot rose and reefer glow.

His injured childhood bullied him.
He skirmished in the Upas trees
and cannibal flowers of the American Dream—

but could not hurt the enemy
powered against him there.

II
Sometimes the dark that gave his life
its cold satanic sheen would shift
a little, and he saw himself
floodlit and eloquent;

yet how could he, "Satan" in The Hole,
guess what the waking dream foretold?

Then false dawn of vision came;
he fell upon his face before
a racist Allah pledged to wrest him from
the hellward-thrusting hands of Calvin's Christ—

to free him and his kind
from Yakub's white-faced treachery.
He rose redeemed from all but prideful anger,

though adulterate attars could not cleanse
him of the odors of the pit.

III
Asalam alaikum!

He X'd his name, became his people's anger,
exhorted them to vengeance for their past;
rebuked, admonished them,

their scourger who
would shame them, drive them from
the lush ice gardens of their servitude.

Asalam alaikum!

Rejecting Ahab, he was of Ahab's tribe.
"Strike through the mask!"

IV

Time. "The martyr's time," he said.
Time and the karate killer,
knifer, gunman. Time that brought
ironic trophies as his faith

twined sparking round the bole,
the fruit of neo-Islam.
"The martyr's time."

But first, the ebb time pilgrimage
toward revelation, hejira to
his final metamorphosis;

Labbayk! Labbayk!

He fell upon his face before
Allah the raceless in whose blazing Oneness all
were one. He rose renewed renamed, became
much more than there was time for him to be.

Words in the Mourning Time

1

For King, for Robert Kennedy,
destroyed by those they could not save,
for King for Kennedy I mourn.
And for America, self-destructive, self-betrayed.

I grieve. Yet know the vanity
of grief—through power of
The Blessed Exile's
transilluminating word

aware of how these deaths, how all
the agonies of our deathbed childbed age
are process, major means whereby,
oh dreadfully, our humanness must be achieved.

II
Lord Riot
      naked
         in flaming clothes
cannibal ruler
       of anger's
          carousals
   sing hey nonny no
terror
   his tribute
       shriek of bloody glass
his praise
   sing wrathful sing vengeful
     sing hey nonny no
gigantic
   and laughing
        sniper on tower
I hate
   I destroy
     I am I am
   sing hey nonny no
   sing burn baby burn

III
and all the atoms cry aloud

I bear Him witness now
Who by the light of suns beyond the suns beyond
    the sun with shrill pen

revealed renewal of
the covenant of timelessness with time, proclaimed
    advent of splendor joy

alone can comprehend
and the imperious evils of an age could not
    withstand and stars

and stones and seas
acclaimed—His life its crystal image and
    magnetic field.

I bear Him witness now—
mystery Whose major clues are the heart of man,
    the mystery of God:

Bahá'u'lláh:
Logos, poet, cosmic hero, surgeon, architect
    of our hope of peace,

wronged, exiled One,
chosen to endure what agonies of knowledge, what
    auroral dark

        bestowals of truth
vision power anguish for our future's sake.
        "I was but a man

        "like others, asleep upon
My couch, when, lo, the breezes of the All-Glorious
        were wafted over Me. . . ."

        Called, as in dead of night
a dreamer is roused to help the helpless flee
        a burning house.

        I bear Him witness now:
toward Him our history in its disastrous quest
        for meaning is impelled.

Monet's "Waterlilies"
(for Bill and Sonja)

Today as the news from Selma and Saigon
poisons the air like fallout,
    I come again to see
the serene great picture that I love.
Here space and time exist in light
the eye like the eye of faith believes.
    The seen, the known
dissolve in irridescence, become
illusive flesh of light
    that was not, was, forever is.

O light beheld as through refracting tears.
Here is the aura of that world
    each of us has lost.
Here is the shadow of its joy.

The Lions

    With what panache, he said,
I bow to the applause,
    I open danger's door
while brasses hold their Ahs
    and set the mood
for courage leonine.
    And in the kingdom-cage
as I make my lions leap,
    through nimbus-fire leap,
oh, as I see them leap—
    unsparing beauty that
creates and serves my will,
    the savage real that clues
my vision of the real—
    my soul exults and Holy cries
and Holy Holy cries, he said.

October

I
October—
its plangency, its glow

as of words in
the poet's mind,

as of God in
the saint's.

II

I wept for your mother
in her pain, wept in
my joy when you were
born,
      Maia,
that October morning.
We named you
for a star a star-like
poem sang.
          I write this
for your birthday
and say I love you
and say October
like the phoenix sings you.

III
This chiming
and tolling
    of lion
and phoenix
and chimera
    colors.
This huntsman's
horn, sounding
    mort for
quarry fleeing
through mirrors
    of burning
into deathless
    dying.

IV
Rockweight
of surprising snow

crushed
the October trees,

broke
branches that

crashing set
the snow on fire.

The Return
(after Pasternak)

Rooms are grotesque with furniture of snow,
ice blisters the hair of portraits;
spiderwebs of snow and ice
are skeleton stars in wolf-wind gloom.

Faces, voices, books we loved.
There were violets in Chinese bowls.
And, ah, the dancers—

They would hunt us down tonight,
they would caper on our graves.
We lived here—when?—under a spell.
We have awakened. We are here.

"Lear Is Gay"
(in memory of Betsy)

That gaiety oh
that gaiety I love
has white hair
or thinning or none,

has limbs askew
often as not,
has dimming sight.
Can manage, can

in fevers, rags,
decreptitude.
And oh can laugh
sometimes

at time as at
a scarecrow whose
hobo shoulders are
a-twitch with crows.

A Plague of Starlings
(Fisk Campus)

Evenings I hear
the workmen fire
into the stiff
magnolia leaves,
routing the starlings
gathered noisy and
befouling there.

Their scissoring
terror like glass
coins spilling breaking
the birds explode
into mica sky
raggedly fall
to ground rigid
in clench of cold.

The spared return,
when the guns are through,
to the spoiled trees
like choiceless poor
to a dangerous
dwelling place,
chitter and quarrel
in the piercing dark
above the killed.

Mornings, I pick
my way past death's
black droppings:
on campus lawns
and streets
the troublesome
starlings
frost-salted lie,
troublesome still.

And if not careful
I shall tread
upon carcasses
carcasses when I
go mornings now
to lecture on
what Socrates,
the hemlock hour nigh,
told sorrowing
Phaedo and the rest
about the migratory
habits of the soul.

IV

A Ballad

of Remembrance

The Diver

Sank through easeful
azure. Flower
creatures flashed and
shimmered there—
lost images
fadingly remembered.
Swiftly descended
into canyon of cold
nightgreen emptiness.
Freefalling, weightless
as in dreams of
wingless flight,
plunged through infra-
space and came to
the dead ship,
carcass that swarmed with
voracious life.
Angelfish, their
lively blue and
yellow prised from
darkness by the
flashlight's beam,
thronged her portholes.
Moss of bryozoans
blurred, obscured her
metal. Snappers,
gold groupers explored her,
fearless of bubbling
manfish. I entered
the wreck, awed by her silence,
feeling more keenly
the iron cold.
With flashlight probing
fogs of water

saw the sad slow
dance of gilded
chairs, the ectoplasmic
swirl of garments,
drowned instruments
of buoyancy,
drunken shoes. Then
livid gesturings,
eldritch hide and
seek of laughing
faces. I yearned to
find those hidden
ones, to fling aside
the mask and call to them,
yield to rapturous
whisperings, have
done with self and
every dinning
vain complexity.
Yet in languid
frenzy strove, as
one freezing fights off
sleep desiring sleep;
strove against the
cancelling arms that
suddenly surrounded
me, fled the numbing
kisses that I craved.
Reflex of life-wish?
Respirator's brittle
belling? Swam from
the ship somehow;
somehow began the
measured rise.

Electrical Storm
(for Arna and Alberta)

God's angry with the world again,
the grey neglected ones would say;
He don't like ugly.
Have mercy, Lord, they prayed,
seeing the lightning's
Mene Mene Tekel,
hearing the preaching thunder's deep
Upharsin.
They hunched up, contracting in corners
away from windows and the dog;
huddled under Jehovah's oldtime wrath,
trusting, afraid.

I huddled too, when a boy,
mindful of things they'd told me
God was bound to make me answer for.
But later I was colleged (as they said)
and learned it was not celestial ire
(Beware the infidels, my son)
but pressure systems,
colliding massive energies
that make a storm.
Well for us. . . .

Last night we drove
through suddenly warring weather.
Wind and lightning havocked,
berserked in wires, trees.
Fallen lines we could not see at first
lay in the yard when we reached home.
The hedge was burning in the rain.

Who knows but what
we might have crossed another sill,
had not our neighbors' warning
kept us from our door?
Who knows if it was heavenly design
or chance
(or knows if there's a difference, after all)
that brought us and our neighbors through—
though others died—
the archetypal dangers of the night?

I know what those
cowering true believers would have said.

Full Moon

No longer throne of a goddess to whom we pray,
no longer the bubble house of childhood's
tumbling Mother Goose man,

The emphatic moon ascends—
the brilliant challenger of rocket experts,
the white hope of communications men.

Some I love who are dead
were watchers of the moon and knew its lore;
planted seeds, trimmed their hair,

Pierced their ears for gold hoop earrings
as it waxed or waned.
It shines tonight upon their graves.

And burned in the garden of Gethsemane,
its light made holy by the dazzling tears
with which it mingled.

And spread its radiance on the exile's path
of Him who was The Glorious One,
its light made holy by His holiness.

Already a mooted goal and tomorrow perhaps
an arms base, a livid sector,
the full moon dominates the dark.

Dawnbreaker

Ablaze
with candles sconced
in weeping eyes
of wounds,

He danced
through jeering streets
to death; oh sang
against

The drumming
mockery God's praise.
Flames nested in
his flesh

Fed the
fires that consume
us now, the fire that
will save.

The Rabbi

Where I grew up, I used to see
the rabbi, dour and pale
in religion's mourner clothes,
walking to the synagogue.

Once there, did he put on
sackcloth and ashes? Wail?
He would not let me in to see
the gold menorah burning.

Mazuzah, Pesach, Chanukah—
these were timbred words I learned,
were things I knew by glimpses.
And I learned schwartze too

And schnapps, which schwartzes bought
on credit from "Jew Baby."
Tippling ironists laughed and said
he'd soon be rich as Rothschild

From their swinish Saturdays.
Hirschel and Molly and I meanwhile
divvied halveh, polly seeds,
were spies and owls and Fu Manchu.

But the synagogue became
New Calvary.
The rabbi bore my friends off
in his prayer shawl.

Belsen, Day of Liberation
(for Rosey)

Her parents and her dolls destroyed,
     her childhood foreclosed,
she watched the foreign soldiers from
     the sunlit window whose black bars

Were crooked crosses inked upon
     her pallid face. "Liebchen,
Liebchen, you should be in bed."
     But she felt ill no longer.

And because that day was a holy day
     when even the dead, it seemed,
must rise, she was allowed to stay
     and see the golden strangers who

Were Father, Brother, and her dream
     of God. Afterwards
she said, "They were so beautiful,
     and they were not afraid."

Approximations

I
In dead of winter
wept beside your open grave.
    Falling snow.

II
Darkness, darkness.
I grope and falter. Flare
    of a match.

III
Not sunflowers, not
roses, but rocks in patterned
    sand grow here. And bloom.

IV
On the platform at
dawn, grey mailbags waiting;
    a crated coffin.

Snow

Smooths and burdens,
endangers, hardens.

Erases, revises.
Extemporizes

Vistas of lunar solitude.
Builds, embellishes a mood.

The Ballad of Sue Ellen Westerfield
(for Clyde)

She grew up in bedeviled southern wilderness,
but had not been a slave, she said,
because her father wept and set her mother free.
She hardened in perilous rivertowns
and after The Surrender,
went as maid upon the tarnished Floating Palaces.
Rivermen reviled her for the rankling cold
sardonic pride
that gave a knife-edge to her comeliness.

When she was old, her back still straight,
her hair still glossy black,
she'd talk sometimes
of dangers lived through on the rivers.
But never told of him,
whose name she'd vowed she would not speak again
till after Jordan.
Oh, he was nearer nearer now
than wearisome kith and kin.
His blue eyes followed her
as she moved about her tasks upon the *Memphis Rose.*
He smiled and joshed, his voice quickening her.
She cursed the circumstance. . . .

The crazing horrors of that summer night,
the swifting flames, he fought his way to her,
the savaging panic, and helped her swim to shore.
The steamer like besieged Atlanta blazing,
the cries, the smoke and bellowing flames,
the flamelit thrashing forms in hellmouth water,
and he swimming out to them,
leaving her dazed and lost.

A woman screaming under the raddled trees—
Sue Ellen felt it was herself who screamed.
The moaning of the hurt, the terrified—
she held off shuddering despair
and went to comfort whom she could.
Wagons torches bells
and whimpering dusk of morning
and blankness lostness nothingness for her
until his arms had lifted her
into wild and secret dark.

How long how long was it they wandered,
loving fearing loving,
fugitives whose dangerous only hidingplace
was love?
How long was it before she knew
she could not forfeit what she was,
even for him—could not, even for him,
forswear her pride?
They kissed and said farewell at last.
He wept as had her father once.
They kissed and said farewell.
Until her dying-bed,
she cursed the circumstance.

Night, Death, Mississippi

I

A quavering cry. Screech-owl?
Or one of them?
The old man in his reek
and gauntness laughs—

One of them, I bet—
and turns out the kitchen lamp,
limping to the porch to listen
in the windowless night.

Be there with Boy and the rest
if I was well again.
Time was. Time was.
White robes like moonlight

In the sweetgum dark.
Unbucked that one then
and him squealing bloody Jesus
as we cut it off.

Time was. A cry?
A cry all right.
He hawks and spits,
fevered as by groinfire.

Have us a bottle,
Boy and me—
he's earned him a bottle—
when he gets home.

Then we beat them, he said,
beat them till our arms was tired
and the big old chains
messy and red.

O Jesus burning on the lily cross

Christ, it was better
than hunting bear
which don't know why
you want him dead.

O night, rawhead and bloodybones night

You kids fetch Paw
some water now so's he
can wash that blood
off him, she said.

O night betrayed by darkness not its own

"An Inference of Mexico"
1. *Day of the Dead*
(Tehuantepec)

The vultures hover wheel and hover
in skies intense as voyeur's gazing.

Cruciform black bells of clay
serenade Mr. and Mrs. Death
exposed in wedding clothes.

> Savage the light upon us,
> savage the light.

The graveblack vultures encircle afternoon,
transformed by steeps of flight
into dark pure images of flight.

> Such pretty girls in Juchitán, señor,
> and if one desires—

Death brings an almond sweetness
to the lips of children playing
with Jack-in-the-tomb and skulls of marzipan.

The tilting vultures glide
through causeway smoke to carrion.

In flowered shirt, androgynous,
the young man under palmleaf knives of sunlight
invites, awaits, obliquely smiles.

> Such pretty girls, señor,
> but if instead—

Barefoot Tehuanas in rhythmic jewels of gold
bear pails of marigolds upon their heads
to the returning dead.

> Flee, amigo, for the dead are angry;
> flee, lest the hands of dead men strike us down,

> and the vultures pick our bones.

2. *Mountains*

Dark as if cloven from darkness
were those mountains.

Night-angled fold on fold
they rose in mist and sunlight,

Their surging darkness
drums bells gongs imploring a god.

3. Veracruz

I

Sunday afternoon,
and couples walk the breakwater
heedless of the bickering spray.
Near the shoreward end,
Indian boys idle and fish.
A shawled brown woman
squinting against
the ricocheting brilliance
of sun and water
shades her eyes and gazes
toward the fort,
fossil of Spanish power,
looming in the harbor.

At the seaward end,
a pharos like a temple rises.
From here the shore
seen across marbling waves
is arabesque ornately green
that hides the inward-falling slum,
the stains and dirty tools of struggle;
appears a destination dreamed of,
never to be reached.

Here only the sea is real—
the barbarous multifoliate sea
with its rustling of leaves,
fire, garments, wind;
its clashing of phantasmal jewels,
its lunar thunder,
animal and human sighing.

Leap now
and cease from error.
Escape. Or shoreward turn,

accepting all—
the losses and farewells,
the long warfare with self,
with God.

The waves roar in and break
roar in and break
with granite spreeing hiss
on bronzegreen rocks below
and glistering upfling of spray.

      II
Thus reality
      bedizened in the warring colors
            of a dream
parades through these
      arcades ornate with music and
            the sea.

Thus reality
      become unbearably a dream
            beckons
out of reach in flyblown streets
      of lapsing rose and purple, dying
            blue.

Thus marimba'd night
      and multifoliate sea become
            phantasmal
space, and there,
      light-years away, one farewell image
            burns and fades and burns.

4. *Idol*
   (Coatlicue, Aztec goddess)

   Wail of the newborn, cry of the dying,
sirenscream of agonies;
   taloned shriek, gong and cymbal of wreckage,
drumbeat of bloodblackened praise;
   soundless drumthrob of the heart wrenched
from the living breast,
   of the raw meaty heart quivering in copal
smoke its praise.

5. *Sub Specie Aeternitatis*

      High amid
gothic rocks the altar stands
that honored once
        a tippling fiercely joyous god.
        Far below,
the empty convent lifts
its cross against a dark
        invasive as the sun
        whose plangent fire
moves like feathered snakes
in trees that shade
        the cloister-garth.

      The curious
may walk the cloister now,
may enter portals barred
        to them no longer
        and wander
hidden passageways and rooms
of stone, meditating on
        such gods as they possess,
        as they have lost.

      Hollow cells
are desolate in their
tranquility
        as relic skulls.
        Arched windows there
look toward the firegreen mountain
resonant with silence of
        a conquered and
        defiant god.

6. Market

Ragged boys
lift sweets, haggle
for acid-green
and bloody gelatins.
A broken smile
dandles its weedy
cigarette
over papayas too ripe
and pyramids
of rotting oranges.
Turkeys like feather-
duster flowers
lie trussed in bunchy smother.
The barefoot cripple
foraging crawls
among rinds, orts,
chewed butts, trampled
peony droppings—
his hunger litany
and suppliant before
altars of mamey,
pineapple, mango.
Turistas pass.
Por caridad, por caridad.
Lord, how they stride
on the hard good legs
money has made them.
Ay! you creatures
who have walked
on seas of money all
your foreign lives!
Por caridad.

Odor of a dripping
carcass moans
beneath the hot
fragrance of carnations,
cool scent of lilies.
Starveling dogs
hover in the reek
of frying; ashy feet
(the twistfoot beggar laughs)
kick at them in vain.
Aloft, the Fire King's
flashing mask of tin
looks down with eyes
of sunstruck glass.

7. *Kid*
   (Cuernavaca)

He is found with the homeless dogs
      that worry sidewalk cafes
where gringos in dollar bills
      deplore and sip. He has

Tricks of pathos for
      the silly foreigners
and so manages not to starve.
      Waiters strike at him and curse;

Deft and quick and accustomed,
      he dances beyond their blows,
taunts them and scampers off,
      laughing as he goes.

8. La Corrida

El toro
From the blind kingdom
where his horns are law,

Gigantically plunging and charging,
he enters the clockface labyrinth—

Man-in-beast, creature
whose guileless power is his doom.

El matador
In the heart of the maze
whose ritual pathways
goading lance, bloodflowering dart,
veronica and sword define,

The fateful one, fate's dazzler,
gleams in suit of lights,
prepares for sensual death
his moment of mocking truth.

In the fiery heart of the maze
the bullgod moves,
transfiguring death
and the wish to die.

Sol y sombra
From all we are yet cannot be
deliver, oh redeem us now.

Of all we know and do not wish
to know, purge oh purge us now.

Olé!

Upon the cross of horns
be crucified for us.

Die for us that death
may call us back to life.

Olé!

A Ballad of Remembrance

Quadroon mermaids, Afro angels, black saints
balanced upon the switchblades of that air
and sang. Tight streets unfolding to the eye
like fans of corrosion and elegiac lace
crackled with their singing: Shadow of time. Shadow of blood.

Shadow, echoed the Zulu king, dangling
from a cluster of balloons. Blood,
whined the gun-metal priestess, floating
over the courtyard where dead men diced.

What will you have? she inquired, the sallow vendeuse
of prepared tarnishes and jokes of nacre and ormolu,
what but those gleamings, oldrose graces,
manners like scented gloves? Contrived ghosts
rapped to metronome clack of lavalieres.

Contrived illuminations riding a threat
of river, masked Negroes wearing chameleon
satins gaudy now as a fortuneteller's
dream of disaster, lighted the crazy flopping
dance of love and hate among joys, rejections.

Accommodate, muttered the Zulu king,
toad on a throne of glaucous poison jewels.
Love, chimed the saints and the angels and the mermaids.
Hate, shrieked the gun-metal priestess
from her spiked bellcollar curved like a fleur-de-lis:

As well have a talon as a finger, a muzzle as a mouth,
as well have a hollow as a heart. And she pinwheeled
away in coruscations of laughter, scattering
those others before her like foil stars.

But the dance continued—now among metaphorical
doors, coffee cups floating poised
hysterias, decors of illusion; now among
mazurka dolls offering death's-heads
of cocaine roses and real violets.

Then you arrived, meditative, ironic,
richly human; and your presence was shore where I rested
released from the hoodoo of that dance, where I spoke
with my true voice again.

And therefore this is not only a ballad of remembrance
for the down-South arcane city with death
in its jaws like gold teeth and archaic cusswords;
not only a token for the troubled generous friends
held in the fists of that schizoid city like flowers,
but also, Mark Van Doren,
a poem of remembrance, a gift, a souvenir for you.

Tour 5

The road winds down through autumn hills
in blazonry of farewell scarlet
and recessional gold,
past cedar groves, through static villages
whose names are all that's left
of Choctaw, Chickasaw.

We stop a moment in a town
watched over by Confederate sentinels,
buy gas and ask directions of a rawboned man
whose eyes revile us as the enemy.

Shrill gorgon silence breathes behind
his taut civility
and in the ever-tautening air,
dark for us despite its Indian summer glow.
We drive on, following the route
of highwaymen and phantoms,

Of slaves and armies.
Children, wordless and remote,
wave at us from kindling porches.
And now the land is flat for miles,
the landscape lush, metallic, flayed,
its brightness harsh as bloodstained swords.

Gulls

In sun-whetted
      morning,
the dropped gull
      splayed
on sand,
      wind
picking at
      its feathers.

Over the headlong
      toppling
rush and leashed-back
      mica'd
fall of the sea,
      gulls
scouting and
      crying.

A Road in Kentucky

And when that ballad lady went
　　　to ease the lover whose life she broke,
oh surely this is the road she took,
　　　road all hackled through barberry fire,
through cedar and alder and sumac and thorn.

Red clay stained her flounces
　　　and stones cut her shoes
and the road twisted on to his loveless house
　　　and his cornfield dying
in the scarecrow's arms.

And when she had left her lover lying
　　　so stark and so stark, with the Star-of-Hope
drawn over his eyes, oh this is the road
　　　that lady walked in the cawing light,
so dark and so dark in the briary light.

Homage to the Empress of the Blues

Because there was a man somewhere in a candystripe silk shirt,
gracile and dangerous as a jaguar and because a woman moaned
for him in sixty-watt gloom and mourned him Faithless Love
Twotiming Love Oh Love Oh Careless Aggravating Love,

> She came out on the stage in yards of pearls, emerging like
> a favorite scenic view, flashed her golden smile and sang.

Because grey laths began somewhere to show from underneath
torn hurdygurdy lithographs of dollfaced heaven;
and because there were those who feared alarming fists of snow
on the door and those who feared the riot-squad of statistics,

> She came out on the stage in ostrich feathers, beaded satin,
> and shone that smile on us and sang.

"The Burly Fading One"

The burly fading one beside the engine,
holding a lantern in his hand,
is Uncle Jed—bullyboy
of wintered recollections now.

Coal miner, stevedore and railroad man,
oh how he brawls and loves,
a Bible over his headlong heart
and no liquor on his breath.

And when he dies, dies not in his own
well-mastered bed but in the waters
of the Johnstown flood, in wild attempt—
so sibling innuendoes all aver—

To save the jolly girl
his wife had mortally wished dead.

"Incense of the Lucky Virgin"

Incense of the Lucky Virgin,
High John the Conqueror
didn't bring him home again,
didn't get his children fed,
      get his children fed.

I prayed and what did prayer avail?
My candles held no power.
An evening came I prayed no more
and blew my candles out,
      oh blew my candles out.

Put on your Sunday ribbon-bows,
Cleola, Willie Mae;
you, Garland, go
and shine your Sunday shoes,
      make haste and shine your shoes.

They were so happy they forgot
they were hungry, daddyless.
Except Cleola maybe—she
wasn't asking, Where we going,
      Mommy, where we going?

Garland was too quick for me
(he didn't yell once as he ran);
Cleola, Willie Mae
won't be hungry any more,
      oh they'll never cry and hunger any more.

Witch Doctor

I

He dines alone surrounded by reflections
of himself. Then after sleep and benzedrine
descends the Cinquecento stair his magic
wrought from hypochondria of the well-
to-do and nagging deathwish of the poor;
swirls on smiling genuflections of
his liveried chauffeur into a crested
lilac limousine, the cynosure
of mousey neighbors tittering behind
Venetian blinds and half afraid of him
and half admiring his outrageous flair.

II

Meanwhile his mother, priestess in gold lamé,
precedes him to the quondam theater
now Israel Temple of the Highest Alpha,
where the bored, the sick, the alien, the tired
await euphoria. With deadly vigor
she prepares the way for mystery
and lucre. Shouts in blues-contralto, "He's
God's dictaphone of all-redeeming truth.
Oh he's the holyweight champeen who's come
to give the knockout lick to your bad luck;
say he's the holyweight champeen who's here
to deal a knockout punch to your hard luck."

III

Reposing on cushions of black leopard skin,
he telephones instructions for a long
slow drive across the park that burgeons now
with spring and sailors. Peers questingly
into the green fountainous twilight, sighs
and turns the gold-plate dial to Music For
Your Dining-Dancing Pleasure. Smoking Egyptian
cigarettes rehearses in his mind
a new device that he must use tonight.

IV

Approaching Israel Temple, mask in place,
he hears ragtime allegros of a "Song
of Zion" that becomes when he appears
a hallelujah wave for him to walk.
His mother and a rainbow-surpliced cordon
conduct him choiring to the altar-stage,
and there he kneels and seems to pray before
a lighted Jesus painted sealskin-brown.
Then with a glittering flourish he arises,
turns, gracefully extends his draperied arms:
"Israelites, true Jews, O found lost tribe
of Israel, receive my blessing now.
Selah, selah." He feels them yearn toward him
as toward a lover, exults before the image
of himself their trust gives back. Stands as though
in meditation, letting their eyes caress
his garments jewelled and chatoyant, cut
to fall, to flow from his tall figure
dramatically just so. Then all at once
he sways, quivers, gesticulates as if
to ward off blows or kisses, and when he speaks
again he utters wildering vocables,
hypnotic no-words planned (and never failing)
to enmesh his flock in theopathic tension.
Cries of eudaemonic pain attest
his artisty. Behind the mask he smiles.
And now in subtly altering light he chants
and sinuously trembles, chants and trembles
while convulsive energies of eager faith
surcharge the theater with power of
their own, a power he has counted on
and for a space allows to carry him.
Dishevelled antiphons proclaim the moment
his followers all day have hungered for,
but which is his alone.

He signals: tambourines begin, frenetic
drumbeat and glissando. He dances from the altar,
robes hissing, flaring, shimmering; down aisles
where mantled guardsmen intercept wild hands
that arduously strain to clutch his vestments,
he dances, dances, ensorcelled and aloof,
the fervid juba of God as lover, healer,
conjurer. And of himself as God.

Mourning Poem for the Queen of Sunday

Lord's lost Him His mockingbird,
His fancy warbler;
Satan sweet-talked her,
four bullets hushed her.
Who would have thought
she'd end that way?

Four bullets hushed her. And the world a-clang with evil.
Who's going to make old hardened sinner men tremble now
and the righteous rock?
Oh who and oh who will sing Jesus down
to help with struggling and doing without and being colored
all through blue Monday?
Till way next Sunday?

All those angels
in their cretonne clouds and finery
the true believer saw
when she rared back her head and sang,
all those angels are surely weeping.
Who would have thought
she'd end that way?

Four holes in her heart. The gold works wrecked.
But she looks so natural in her big bronze coffin
among the Broken Hearts and Gates-Ajar,
it's as if any moment she'd lift her head
from its pillow of chill gardenias
and turn this quiet into shouting Sunday
and make folks forget what she did on Monday.

Oh, Satan sweet-talked her,
and four bullets hushed her.
Lord's lost Him His diva,
His fancy warbler's gone.
Who would have thought,
who would have thought she'd end that way?

"Summertime and the Living . . . ."

Nobody planted roses, he recalls,
but sunflowers gangled there sometimes,
tough-stalked and bold
and like the vivid children there unplanned.
There circus-poster horses curveted
in trees of heaven
above the quarrels and shattered glass,
and he was bareback rider of them all.

No roses there in summer—
oh, never roses except when people died—
and no vacations for his elders,
so harshened after each unrelenting day
that they were shouting-angry.
But summer was, they said, the poor folks' time
of year. And he remembers
how they would sit on broken steps amid

The fevered tossings of the dusk, the dark,
wafting hearsay with funeral-parlor fans
or making evening solemn by
their quietness. Feels their Mosaic eyes
upon him, though the florist roses
that only sorrow could afford
long since have bidden them Godspeed.

Oh, summer summer summertime—

Then grim street preachers shook
their tambourines and Bibles in the face
of tolerant wickedness;
then Elks parades and big splendiferous
Jack Johnson in his diamond limousine
set the ghetto burgeoning
with fantasies
of Ethiopia spreading her gorgeous wings.

The Whipping

The old woman across the way
      is whipping the boy again
and shouting to the neighborhood
      her goodness and his wrongs.

Wildly he crashes through elephant ears,
      pleads in dusty zinnias,
while she in spite of crippling fat
      pursues and corners him.

She strikes and strikes the shrilly circling
      boy till the stick breaks
in her hand. His tears are rainy weather
      to woundlike memories:

My head gripped in bony vise
      of knees, the writhing struggle
to wrench free, the blows, the fear
      worse than blows that hateful

Words could bring, the face that I
      no longer knew or loved . . . .
Well, it is over now, it is over,
      and the boy sobs in his room,

And the woman leans muttering against
      a tree, exhausted, purged—
avenged in part for lifelong hidings
      she has had to bear.

Those Winter Sundays

Sundays too my father got up early
and put his clothes on in the blueblack cold,
then with cracked hands that ached
from labor in the weekday weather made
banked fires blaze. No one ever thanked him.

I'd wake and hear the cold splintering, breaking.
When the rooms were warm, he'd call,
and slowly I would rise and dress,
fearing the chronic angers of that house,

Speaking indifferently to him,
who had driven out the cold
and polished my good shoes as well.
What did I know, what did I know
of love's austere and lonely offices?

Perseus

Her sleeping head with its great gelid mass
      of serpents torpidly astir
burned into the mirroring shield—
      a scathing image dire
as hated truth the mind accepts at last
      and festers on.
I struck. The shield flashed bare.

Yet even as I lifted up the head
      and started from that place
of gazing silences and terrored stone,
      I thirsted to destroy.
None could have passed me then—
      no garland-bearing girl, no priest
or staring boy—and lived.

Theme and Variation
(for Erma)

I

Fossil, fuschia, mantis, man,
fire and water, earth and air—
all things alter even as I behold,
all things alter, the stranger said.

Alter, become a something more,
a something less. Are the revelling shadows
of a changing permanence. Are, are not
and same and other, the stranger said.

II

I sense, he said, the lurking rush, the sly
transience flickering at the edge of things.
I've spied from the corner of my eye
upon the striptease of reality.

There is, there is, he said, an imminence
that turns to curiosa all I know;
that changes light to rainbow darkness
wherein God waylays us and empowers.

"From the Corpse Woodpiles, from the Ashes"

From the corpse woodpiles, from the ashes
and staring pits of Dachau,
Buchenwald they come—

O David, Hirschel, Eva,
cops and robbers with me once,
their faces are like yours—

From Johannesburg, from Seoul.
Their struggles are all horizons.
Their deaths encircle me.

Through target streets I run,
in light part nightmare
and part vision fleeing

What I cannot flee, and reach
that cold cloacal cell
where He, who is man beatified

And Godly mystery,
lies chained, His pain
our anguish and our anodyne.

Bahá'u'lláh in the Garden of Ridwan

Agonies confirm His hour,
      and swords like compass-needles turn
            toward His heart.

The midnight air is forested
      with presences that shelter Him
            and sheltering praise

The auroral darkness which is God
      and sing the word made flesh again
            in Him,

Eternal exile whose return
      epiphanies repeatedly
            foretell.

He watches in a borrowed garden,
      prays. And sleepers toss upon
            their armored beds,

Half-roused by golden knocking at
      the doors of consciousness. Energies
            like angels dance

Glorias of recognition.
      Within the rock the undiscovered suns
            release their light.

Middle Passage

I

Jesús, Estrella, Esperanza, Mercy:

> Sails flashing to the wind like weapons,
> sharks following the moans the fever and the dying;
> horror the corposant and compass rose.

Middle Passage:
>> voyage through death
>>> to life upon these shores.

> "10 April 1800—
> Blacks rebellious. Crew uneasy. Our linguist says
> their moaning is a prayer for death,
> ours and their own. Some try to starve themselves.
> Lost three this morning leaped with crazy laughter
> to the waiting sharks, sang as they went under."

Desire, Adventure, Tartar, Ann:

> Standing to America, bringing home
> black gold, black ivory, black seed.

>> *Deep in the festering hold thy father lies,*
>> *of his bones New England pews are made,*
>> *those are altar lights that were his eyes.*

Jesus   Saviour   Pilot   Me
Over   Life's   Tempestuous   Sea

We pray that Thou wilt grant, O Lord,
safe passage to our vessels bringing
heathen souls unto Thy chastening.

Jesus   Saviour

"8 bells. I cannot sleep, for I am sick
with fear, but writing eases fear a little
since still my eyes can see these words take shape
upon the page & so I write, as one
would turn to exorcism. 4 days scudding,
but now the sea is calm again. Misfortune
follows in our wake like sharks (our grinning
tutelary gods). Which one of us
has killed an albatross? A plague among
our blacks—Ophthalmia: blindness—& we
have jettisoned the blind to no avail.
It spreads, the terrifying sickness spreads.
Its claws have scratched sight from the Capt.'s eyes
& there is blindness in the fo'c'sle
& we must sail 3 weeks before we come
to port."

> *What port awaits us, Davy Jones'*
> *or home? I've heard of slavers drifting, drifting,*
> *playthings of wind and storm and chance, their crews*
> *gone blind, the jungle hatred*
> *crawling up on deck.*

Thou   Who   Walked   On   Galilee

"Deponent further sayeth *The Bella J*
left the Guinea Coast
with cargo of five hundred blacks and odd
for the barracoons of Florida:

"That there was hardly room 'tween-decks for half
the sweltering cattle stowed spoon-fashion there;
that some went mad of thirst and tore their flesh
and sucked the blood:

"That Crew and Captain lusted with the comeliest
of the savage girls kept naked in the cabins;
that there was one they called The Guinea Rose
and they cast lots and fought to lie with her:

"That when the Bo's'n piped all hands, the flames
spreading from starboard already were beyond
control, the negroes howling and their chains
entangled with the flames:

"That the burning blacks could not be reached,
that the Crew abandoned ship,
leaving their shrieking negresses behind,
that the Captain perished drunken with the wenches:

"Further Deponent sayeth not."

Pilot   Oh   Pilot   Me

    II
Aye, lad, and I have seen those factories,
Gambia, Rio Pongo, Calabar;
have watched the artful mongos baiting traps
of war wherein the victor and the vanquished

Were caught as prizes for our barracoons.
Have seen the nigger kings whose vanity
and greed turned wild black hides of Fellatah,
Mandingo, Ibo, Kru to gold for us.

And there was one—King Anthracite we named him—
fetish face beneath French parasols
of brass and orange velvet, impudent mouth
whose cups were carven skulls of enemies:

He'd honor us with drum and feast and conjo
and palm-oil-glistening wenches deft in love,
and for tin crowns that shone with paste,
red calico and German-silver trinkets

Would have the drums talk war and send
his warriors to burn the sleeping villages
and kill the sick and old and lead the young
in coffles to our factories.

Twenty years a trader, twenty years,
for there was wealth aplenty to be harvested
from those black fields, and I'd be trading still
but for the fevers melting down my bones.

III

Shuttles in the rocking loom of history,
the dark ships move, the dark ships move,
their bright ironical names
like jests of kindness on a murderer's mouth;
plough through thrashing glister toward
fata morgana's lucent melting shore,
weave toward New World littorals that are
mirage and myth and actual shore.

Voyage through death,
                    voyage whose chartings are unlove.

A charnel stench, effluvium of living death·
spreads outward from the hold,
where the living and the dead, the horribly dying,
lie interlocked, lie foul with blood and excrement.

> *Deep in the festering hold thy father lies,*
> *the corpse of mercy rots with him,*
> *rats eat love's rotten gelid eyes.*

But, oh, the living look at you
with human eyes whose suffering accuses you,
whose hatred reaches through the swill of dark
to strike you like a leper's claw.

You cannot stare that hatred down
or chain the fear that stalks the watches
and breathes on you its fetid scorching breath;
cannot kill the deep immortal human wish,
the timeless will.

> "But for the storm that flung up barriers
> of wind and wave, *The Amistad,* señores,
> would have reached the port of Príncipe in two,
> three days at most; but for the storm we should
> have been prepared for what befell.
> Swift as the puma's leap it came. There was
> that interval of moonless calm filled only
> with the water's and the rigging's usual sounds,
> then sudden movement, blows and snarling cries
> and they had fallen on us with machete
> and marlinspike. It was as though the very
> air, the night itself were striking us.
> Exhausted by the rigors of the storm,
> we were no match for them. Our men went down
> before the murderous Africans. Our loyal
> Celestino ran from below with gun
> and lantern and I saw, before the cane-
> knife's wounding flash, Cinquez,
> that surly brute who calls himself a prince,
> directing, urging on the ghastly work.
> He hacked the poor mulatto down, and then
> he turned on me. The decks were slippery
> when daylight finally came. It sickens me
> to think of what I saw, of how these apes
> threw overboard the butchered bodies of
> our men, true Christians all, like so much jetsam.

Enough, enough. The rest is quickly told:
Cinquez was forced to spare the two of us
you see to steer the ship to Africa,
and we like phantoms doomed to rove the sea
voyaged east by day and west by night,
deceiving them, hoping for rescue,
prisoners on our own vessel, till
at length we drifted to the shores of this
your land, America, where we were freed
from our unspeakable misery. Now we
demand, good sirs, the extradition of
Cinquez and his accomplices to La
Havana. And it distresses us to know
there are so many here who seem inclined
to justify the mutiny of these blacks.
We find it paradoxical indeed
that you whose wealth, whose tree of liberty
are rooted in the labor of your slaves
should suffer the august John Quincy Adams
to speak with so much passion of the right
of chattel slaves to kill their lawful masters
and with his Roman rhetoric weave a hero's
garland for Cinquez. I tell you that
we are determined to return to Cuba
with our slaves and there see justice done. Cinquez—
or let us say 'the Prince'—Cinquez shall die."

The deep immortal human wish,
the timeless will:

　　Cinquez its deathless primaveral image,
　　life that transfigures many lives.

Voyage through death
　　　　　　　　to life upon these shores.

O Daedalus, Fly Away Home
(For Maia and Julie)

Drifting night in the Georgia pines,
coonskin drum and jubilee banjo.
    Pretty Malinda, dance with me.

Night is juba, night is conjo.
    Pretty Malinda, dance with me.

Night is an African juju man
weaving a wish and a weariness together
    to make two wings.

    O fly away home fly away

Do you remember Africa?

    O cleave the air fly away home

My gran, he flew back to Africa,
just spread his arms and
    flew away home.

Drifting night in the windy pines;
night is a laughing, night is a longing.
    Pretty Malinda, come to me.

Night is a mourning juju man
weaving a wish and a weariness together
    to make two wings.

    O fly away home fly away

The Ballad of Nat Turner

Then fled, O brethren, the wicked juba
        and wandered wandered far
from curfew joys in the Dismal's night.
        Fool of St. Elmo's fire

In scary night I wandered, praying,
        Lord God my harshener,
speak to me now or let me die;
        speak, Lord, to this mourner.

And came at length to livid trees
        where Ibo warriors
hung shadowless, turning in wind
        that moaned like Africa,

Their belltongue bodies dead, their eyes
        alive with the anger deep
in my own heart. Is this the sign,
        the sign forepromised me?

The spirits vanished. Afraid and lonely
        I wandered on in blackness.
Speak to me now or let me die.
        Die, whispered the blackness.

And wild things gasped and scuffled in
        the night; seething shapes
of evil frolicked upon the air.
        I reeled with fear, I prayed.

Sudden brightness clove the preying
        darkness, brightness that was
itself a golden darkness, brightness
        so bright that it was darkness.

And there were angels, their faces hidden
        from me, angels at war
with one another, angels in dazzling
        combat. And oh the splendor,

The fearful splendor of that warring.
        Hide me, I cried to rock and bramble.
Hide me, the rock, the bramble cried. . . .
        How tell you of that holy battle?

The shock of wing on wing and sword
        on sword was the tumult of
a taken city burning. I cannot
        say how long they strove,

For the wheel in a turning wheel which is time
        in eternity had ceased
its whirling, and owl and moccasin,
        panther and nameless beast

And I were held like creatures fixed
        in flaming, in fiery amber.
But I saw I saw oh many of
        those mighty beings waver,

Waver and fall, go streaking down
        into swamp water, and the water
hissed and steamed and bubbled and locked
        shuddering shuddering over

The fallen and soon was motionless.
        Then that massive light
began a-folding slowly in
        upon itself, and I

Beheld the conqueror faces and, lo,
    they were like mine, I saw
they were like mine and in joy and terror
    wept, praising praising Jehovah.

Oh praised my honer, harshener
    till a sleep came over me,
a sleep heavy as death. And when
    I awoke at last free

And purified, I rose and prayed
    and returned after a time
to the blazing fields, to the humbleness.
    And bided my time.

Runagate Runagate

I.

Runs falls rises stumbles on from darkness into darkness
and the darkness thicketed with shapes of terror
and the hunters pursuing and the hounds pursuing
and the night cold and the night long and the river
to cross and the jack-muh-lanterns beckoning beckoning
and blackness ahead and when shall I reach that somewhere
morning and keep on going and never turn back and keep on going

       Runagate
           Runagate
              Runagate

Many thousands rise and go
many thousands crossing over

               O mythic North
            O star-shaped yonder Bible city

Some go weeping and some rejoicing
some in coffins and some in carriages
some in silks and some in shackles

       Rise and go or fare you well

No more auction block for me
no more driver's lash for me

       If you see my Pompey, 30 yrs of age,
       new breeches, plain stockings, negro shoes;
       if you see my Anna, likely young mulatto
       branded E on the right cheek, R on the left,
       catch them if you can and notify subscriber.
       Catch them if you can, but it won't be easy.
       They'll dart underground when you try to catch them,
       plunge into quicksand, whirlpools, mazes,
       turn into scorpions when you try to catch them.

And before I'll be a slave
I'll be buried in my grave

    North star and bonanza gold
    I'm bound for the freedom, freedom-bound
    and oh Susyanna don't you cry for me

        Runagate

        Runagate

II.
Rises from their anguish and their power,

        Harriet Tubman,

        woman of earth, whipscarred,
        a summoning, a shining

        Mean to be free

    And this was the way of it, brethren brethren,
    way we journeyed from Can't to Can.
    Moon so bright and no place to hide,
    the cry up and the patterollers riding,
    hound dogs belling in bladed air.
    And fear starts a-murbling, Never make it,
    we'll never make it. *Hush that now,*
    and she's turned upon us, levelled pistol
    glinting in the moonlight:
    Dead folks can't jaybird-talk, she says;
    you keep on going now or die, she says.

Wanted   Harriet Tubman   alias The General
alias Moses   Stealer of Slaves

In league with Garrison   Alcott   Emerson
Garrett   Douglass   Thoreau   John Brown

Armed and known to be Dangerous

Wanted   Reward   Dead or Alive

    Tell me, Ezekiel, oh tell me do you see
    mailed Jehovah coming to deliver me?

Hoot-owl calling in the ghosted air,
five times calling to the hants in the air.
Shadow of a face in the scary leaves,
shadow of a voice in the talking leaves:

    Come ride-a my train

    Oh that train, ghost-story train
    through swamp and savanna movering movering,
    over trestles of dew, through caves of the wish,
    Midnight Special on a sabre track movering movering,
    first stop Mercy and the last Hallelujah.

    Come ride-a my train

      Mean mean mean to be free.

Frederick Douglass

When it is finally ours, this freedom, this liberty, this beautiful
and terrible thing, needful to man as air,
usable as earth; when it belongs at last to all,
when it is truly instinct, brain matter, diastole, systole,
reflex action; when it is finally won; when it is more
than the gaudy mumbo jumbo of politicians:
this man, this Douglass, this former slave, this Negro
beaten to his knees, exiled, visioning a world
where none is lonely, none hunted, alien,
this man, superb in love and logic, this man
shall be remembered. Oh, not with statues' rhetoric,
not with legends and poems and wreaths of bronze alone,
but with the lives grown out of his life, the lives
fleshing his dream of the beautiful, needful thing.